HANDLING DISCIPLINE

Tricia Jackson BA, MSc (Personnel Management), MInstAM, FCIPD is a freelance training and personnel consultant. Tricia has many years' experience as a generalist practitioner in both the public and private sectors. She is currently involved in identifying and providing training solutions, personnel consultancy, tutoring on CIPD programmes and competence assessment. Tricia is the co-author, with Malcolm Martin, of the CIPD's recommended textbook for the Certificate in Personnel Practice (*Personnel Practice*, M. Martin and T. Jackson, 2nd edn, CIPD, 2000) and author of four other CIPD Good Practice titles: *Drugs and Alcohol Policies* (1999), *Smoking Policies* (1999), *Career Development* (2000) and *Handling Grievances* (2000). Tricia lives in Weybridge, Surrey.

The Chartered Institute of Personnel and Development is the leading publisher of books and reports for personnel and training professionals, students, and all those concerned with the effective management and development of people at work. For details of all our titles, please contact the Publishing Department:

tel 020-8263 3387

fax 020-8263 3850

e-mail publish@cipd.co.uk

The catalogue of all CIPD titles can be viewed on the CIPD website:

www.cipd.co.uk/publications

HANDLING
DISCIPLINE

TRICIA JACKSON

CHARTERED INSTITUTE OF PERSONNEL AND DEVELOPMENT

© Tricia Jackson 2001

First published 2001

Design and typesetting by
Wyvern 21, Bristol

Printed in Great Britain by the Short Run Press, Exeter

British Library Cataloguing-in-Publication Data
A catalogue record for this book is available
from the British Library

ISBN 0-85292-930-7

Chartered Institute of Personnel and Development, CIPD House,
Camp Road, London SW19 4UX
Tel: 020-8971 9000 Fax: 020-8263 3333
E-mail: cipd@cipd.co.uk
Website: www.cipd.co.uk
Incorporated by Royal Charter. Registered charity no. 1079797.

Contents

Acknowledgements

This book had a very lengthy conception so it is difficult to remember all those who have contributed to its contents, either expressly or inadvertently. May I first express my gratitude to my current and recent students and clients who have kept me up to date with real twenty-first-century disciplinary and capability issues – hence the reason that the case studies in this book are not confined to clock-card offences, skylarking and failures to follow sickness absence notification procedures.

Special thanks are due to Matthew Reisz of CIPD Enterprises for his editorial input and words of encouragement. I would also like to express my thanks to the people who have given permission for the use of their company materials: Katherine Tickle of Barbour Index and Kevin Rampling of Reigate and Banstead Council.

Introduction

Introduction

According to the ACAS Code of Practice:[1]

> Disciplinary issues arise when problems of conduct
> or capability are identified by the employer and
> management seeks to address them through well-
> recognised procedures.

It is an inevitable fact that, from time to time, disciplinary incidents will occur in the workplace. They may result from a number of factors, including poor working relationships, employees' personal circumstances impinging on their working lives, unreasonable requests from managers and general employee discontent.

Managers have a right to discipline employees when their behaviour threatens the mutual trust and confidence that is necessary for the employment relationship to exist.

1

Organisations must, however, have well-designed disciplinary rules and procedures, and managers must have been trained in their operation in order for the outcomes to be satisfactory.

In this opening chapter we examine common disciplinary problems and the differences between conduct and capability issues. We suggest that, except for the smallest employers, organisations should set up separate disciplinary and capability procedures to reflect the differences in the appropriate handling of these issues.

In Chapter 2 we consider why organisations need formal procedures to deal with discipline and capability. This is linked to the legal obligations on employers covered in Chapter 3. In Chapters 4–6 we look at the design and implementation of disciplinary and capability policies and procedures. Chapter 7 concentrates on good practices in carrying out investigations and in conducting disciplinary interviews and appeals hearings. The concluding chapters provide a summary of the key issues and details of further reading and useful contacts. Throughout the book we use real case studies to demonstrate the key learning points

Who should read this book?

The book is primarily aimed at those who are responsible for formulating and reviewing disciplinary procedures and those who handle conduct and capability issues in the workplace. This is likely to include line managers at all levels up to the most senior, as well as personnel specialists, trade union/employee representatives and other third parties. The book should also prove useful to any employees who want to understand more about fair procedures and their rights.

Common disciplinary problems

Employers are likely to experience a range of disciplinary problems. The most common ones include:

- poor timekeeping and unauthorised absence
- misuse of company facilities
- failure to follow instructions
- failure to meet targets and deadlines
- breaches of company policies
- attitudinal problems, possibly because of personality clashes
- breaches of confidentiality
- insubordination.

On the other hand, work performance or capability problems may arise because of:

- long-term absence due to sickness
- frequent short-term sickness absences
- a lack of proper qualifications to do the job
- incompetence.

Conduct v capability

Disciplinary procedures are usually designed to deal with misconduct and may be inappropriate for capability issues, especially where the reason for the shortfall in performance is not within the employee's control. For instance, is it appropriate to discipline:

- employees when they have been absent due to sickness?
- a salesman for failing to meet his sales targets when he has not received adequate training and supervision?
- a technician for her lack of proper qualifications to do the job when this resulted from a change in job content?
- employees whose shortfalls in performance are due to negligence, lack of application or attitudinal problems?

The answer to the first three questions is 'no', and to the fourth is 'yes'. Thus, in poor performance cases, investigation will first need to determine the reasons for the shortfalls.

To accommodate this difference in approach, we strongly urge that a separate capability procedure is designed to cover issues of ill-health and poor performance for reasons outside of the employee's control. This procedure would bear some similarities to a disciplinary procedure but would differ in the steps taken to resolve the problem – see Chapters 4 and 5 for more information.

> Please note that throughout this book we often use the term 'disciplinary procedure' in a generic sense.

Reference

1 ACAS. *Code of Practice 1: Disciplinary and Grievance Procedures*. p5. London, ACAS, 2000.

Why do we need a formal procedure?

Aim

Disciplinary procedures should not be viewed primarily as a means of imposing sanctions or a route to dismissing employees legally. The aim is rather to help and encourage improvement amongst employees whose conduct or standard of work is unsatisfactory. Thus a correctional, rather than a punitive, approach should be adopted.

Benefits

It is in everybody's interest to have a disciplined and well-organised workforce, and fair and efficient handling of disciplinary incidents can significantly contribute towards harmonious relations. Thus a formal policy and procedure needs to be in place, backed up by good management practices, to ensure consistency and a co-ordinated approach. This will bring the following benefits for the organisation and employees:

- It helps employees understand the organisational rules and standards of conduct and performance expected of them.
- It provides a fair and speedy means of dealing with disciplinary incidents.
- It helps promote the organisation's values and better day-to-day management practices.
- It assists employees in developing their potential in line with organisational values, thus enhancing their employability.
- It reduces the likelihood of losing employees who have the potential to improve.
- It saves employers time and money, as issues that may be undermining employee morale are identified and corrected.
- It provides a better defence in employment tribunal cases.
- It helps to build an organisational climate based on openness and trust.

Poor handling of discipline

What if you do not have a well-designed procedure or your managers are inept in their handling of disciplinary situations? The examples below illustrate some of the potential dangers:

1 A female employee was convicted for drinking and

driving. The manager followed the correct procedure but decided to issue only a written warning and made changes to the job role to accommodate the driving ban. This sanction was viewed as too lenient by other employees, who felt that management was weak and unwilling to impose the company rules. It also set a precedent for those involved in similar future incidents.

2 A recently appointed employee was dismissed for poor performance, despite regularly asking for the IT training necessary to enable him to do his job. Colleagues felt that the manager should have responded to such a reasonable request and was overly harsh in his decision. This led to discontent and demotivation in the team, and the ex-employee subsequently submitted a breach-of-contract claim.

3 A supervisor failed to carry out a full investigation into an incident that involved employees playing a practical joke on a colleague. She decided to issue six of her team with written warnings even though only four were guilty. The other two were frustrated and disillusioned by the fact that their honesty had been questioned and that their previously unblemished records had not been taken into account. This damage to working relationships proved too difficult to repair and both employees left the company shortly afterwards.

4 A manager, after issuing a series of warnings, dismissed an employee for poor timekeeping. A claim for unfair dismissal followed. At the employment tribunal, the manager found that much of his

evidence was disputed by the ex-employee and, as he had not kept notes and adequate records, was unable to defend his actions. The company lost the case.

5 An employee was given a final written warning for excessive personal use of the Internet and this penalty was upheld at the appeals stage. Yet the manager hearing the appeal failed to take account of the employee's contention that there was no written company policy on Internet usage and that this offence was not mentioned in the disciplinary rules, which had not been updated for many years. The employee felt that he had been singled out for punishment though others were guilty of the same offence. He submitted a formal grievance, also alleging racial discrimination, which took many hours of management time before it was satisfactorily resolved.

6 A claim of unfair dismissal was made by an ex-employee who argued that her dismissal for inappropriate behaviour at a Christmas party was an excessive response. She further contended that she was denied her right of accompaniment and appeal in the internal disciplinary proceedings. As a matter of principle and to convey a message to other employees that such behaviour could not be tolerated, the managing director decided to fight the claim, although it proved to be costly and time-consuming. In the event, the company lost; the experience did little to enhance its reputation in the eyes of employees and customers.

The message

The message is clear. Organisations without formal written disciplinary procedures are strongly advised to introduce them, and all other organisations, unionised and non-unionised, should consider whether they ought to:

- revise their disciplinary rules to include clearer definitions of what will be viewed as inappropriate conduct and behaviour (see Chapter 4)
- revise their disciplinary procedures in line with the new ACAS Code of Practice and new statutory right of accompaniment (see Chapters 3 and 4)
- develop training programmes for managers on how to discipline employees and keep accurate records (see Chapter 7)
- consider introducing separate capability procedures (see Chapter 5).

Such changes should, however, be introduced as part of an integrated approach to effective performance management. The management strategy should aim to create a positive environment of mutual respect and trust where employees:

- are given clear guidelines and involved in agreeing performance standards
- understand the likely consequences should they fail to meet standards or abide by the rules
- opt to raise concerns via the grievance procedure rather than disobeying instructions they do not agree with.

9

This preventive approach is based on the principle that disciplinary incidents can be averted by good people management practices. Organisations need to select the right people in the first place, provide effective induction and on-the-job training, install sensible retention strategies that develop, reward and motivate employees, and use appropriate communications and employee involvement mechanisms. All of these create an excellent foundation to enable disciplinary procedures to operate effectively.

3

What rights and duties does the law provide?

The legal position

Employers are not specifically required by law to have written disciplinary procedures in place. There are, however, a number of compelling arguments to support the case for formal disciplinary procedures within all employing organisations, as will soon become clear when we examine the relevant statutes, the recently revised ACAS Code of Practice and the lessons from case law.

Employment Rights Act 1996

Many individual employment rights were consolidated into the Employment Rights Act 1996; the main one of interest here is the right not to be unfairly dismissed, which is applicable to employees with one year's service or more. When hearing unfair dismissal cases, employment tribunals will expect the employer to show:

- the reason for dismissal and that this was related to the employee's conduct
- that they acted reasonably in treating this as a sufficient reason to dismiss the employee.

Thus employment tribunals will seek to determine whether the reason was a fair and sufficient one, warranting dismissal, and whether the employer acted consistently in relation to previous similar incidents. The tribunal will further check whether the employer followed a correct procedure.

The Employment Rights Act also requires employers with 20 or more employees to provide them with a written statement specifying the main terms and conditions of their employment. These particulars must specify any disciplinary rules applicable to them and indicate the person to whom they should apply if they are dissatisfied with a disciplinary decision. The statement should also explain any further steps that exist in the procedure for dealing with disciplinary decisions. The disciplinary procedure itself does not have to be provided as part of the statement but should be reasonably accessible to the employee.

Employment Relations Act 1999

The Employment Relations Act (ERA) 1999 requires employers to permit workers to be accompanied at specified disciplinary and grievance meetings. This clause came into effect in September 2000. In summary, the main provisions relating to disciplinary matters are as follows:

- The right extends to workers and not just employees working under a contract of employment. Thus self-employed people who do not run their own business, homeworkers and agency workers are also included.
- The right applies to hearings that could result in a formal warning to the worker (whether about conduct or capability) or to the employer taking action such as suspension without pay, demotion or dismissal, confirmation of a warning already issued or some other action taken. The section on the ACAS Code below provides some clarification of what this means in practice, but a cautious approach is advisable to avoid disputes and the

danger of being sidetracked from the purpose of the disciplinary hearing.

- Workers will be protected against victimisation or dismissal in connection with this right, ie they will be able to complain to employment tribunals of both unfair dismissal and detrimental treatment.
- The accompanying person may be a fellow worker, a full-time or a lay trade union official. This right applies equally to workers in unionised and non-unionised environments.
- The employer may need to postpone the hearing if the chosen companion is not available.
- Fellow workers and lay trade union officials should be allowed a reasonable amount of paid time off to fulfil their duties.
- The chosen companion may address the hearing, ask questions and confer privately with the worker but has no legal right to answer questions on behalf of the worker.
- Failure to allow a worker to be accompanied or to rearrange a hearing to accommodate the worker's companion may result in a complaint to an employment tribunal and a compensation award of up to two weeks' pay.

Please note that in this book we are using the terms 'employee' and 'worker' interchangeably, but they do have separate and specific meanings under employment law.

ACAS Code of Practice

The ACAS Code of Practice on Disciplinary and Grievance Procedures (2000) contains practical guidance for employers, workers and their representatives or companions on the statutory provisions above. Although the Code has no direct legal force, rulings by the Employment Appeal Tribunal (EAT) have stated that it should form the basis upon which an employer's conduct is judged by an employment tribunal and that it points the way towards sound employment relations practice.

The Code is divided into three sections:

- Section 1 deals with disciplinary practice and procedures.
- Section 2 considers the handling of grievances.
- Section 3 is concerned with the statutory right of accompaniment at disciplinary and grievance hearings.

We rely heavily on the Section 1 provisions in Chapter 4 and throughout this book. With respect to the right of accompaniment, the Code offers the following advice:

- There is no right to be accompanied at an informal interview or counselling session unless it becomes clear during such a meeting that disciplinary action may be necessary. In such an event, the meeting should be terminated and a formal hearing convened, at which the worker should be afforded the statutory right of accompaniment.
- There is similarly no right to be accompanied during an investigation into the facts of a

disciplinary case. This distinction highlights the
need to separate investigatory and disciplinary
meetings.

Further assistance in ensuring compliance with the new
right of accompaniment is contained in the ACAS Code.

Natural justice

Disciplinary procedures need to adhere to the rules of natural justice. In summary these are as follows:

- The employee charged with misconduct should be
  informed, in advance, that a disciplinary hearing
  is taking place.
- There should be a full investigation by an
  unbiased individual to establish the facts of the
  case.
- At the hearing, the employee should be informed
  of the precise allegations and given an
  opportunity to answer them.
- Those conducting the disciplinary hearing should
  keep an open mind and not prejudge the case.
- The employee is entitled to appeal against a
  disciplinary decision to a third party who has not
  previously been involved in the case.
- The employee should be allowed to challenge any
  evidence that will be relied upon in reaching a
  disciplinary decision.

The following case study illustrates this last point.

> **Case study 1 – the employee must be privy to the evidence against him or her**
>
> A fertiliser manufacturer dismissed an employee for gross misconduct. He was accused of fabricating a dog guard from company materials and fitting it to the back seat of his Land Rover during working hours. In his defence, he claimed that the materials were waste products and that he had worked on the dog guard only during break times. The company knew that they were on fairly safe ground as they had video evidence to show that the latter contention was untrue. Their downfall was that they did not reveal this evidence to the employee during the internal disciplinary proceedings so he was unable to put his side of the story. The employment tribunal found that the dismissal had been unfair because of this and other procedural deficiencies. (Since, like the employer, they found the employee to be unconvincing, however, they did reduce his compensation by 90 per cent.)

The remaining chapters provide guidance on how to ensure that these points are covered, both in disciplinary procedures and wider management practices.

Contractually binding procedures

In some organisations disciplinary procedures are incorporated into the employees' contracts of employment. This means that, where the procedure specifies the number of stages of hearings and appeals, time frames and disciplinary panel membership, any departure from this may result in a breach-of-contract claim. This right applies to all employees, regardless of their length of service.

Further, once incorporated, such procedures are difficult to change.

It is therefore preferable for employers not to have contractually binding procedures. To avoid this, procedures should contain wording to this effect:

> This procedure is for guidance only and does not form part of the employee's contractual rights. Furthermore, its contents may be revised from time to time.

Overlap with grievance procedures

The ACAS Code provides clarification on another important question: what happens when grievances are raised at the same time as disciplinary issues?

If employers have separate procedures for handling grievances and discipline, they will want appeals against disciplinary decisions to be channelled through the disciplinary appeals procedure, not the grievance procedure. However, an employee may wish to raise a grievance about the way in which a manager handled a disciplinary matter or conducted the investigation. An employee in this position has a right to seek redress even when facing disciplinary charges. Employers must therefore observe both sets of procedural rules.

The ACAS Code suggests that it may be appropriate to suspend the disciplinary procedure for a short period to allow the grievance to be heard. Furthermore, consideration might be given to bringing in another manager to deal with the disciplinary case.

Associated legislation

Here we consider associated legislation that has an impact on the design and operation of disciplinary procedures.

Employment Rights (Dispute Resolution) Act 1998

The Employment Rights (Dispute Resolution) Act 1998 introduced the means by which ACAS could establish a voluntary arbitration scheme. This is a way of resolving a dispute in which an arbitrator's decision is binding as a matter of law and has the same effect as a court or tribunal judgement. The scheme is intended to be a fair, impartial, speedy and credible alternative to the employment tribunal system. It came into effect in May 2001 and it is too early to judge its likely long-term impact. The main features of the scheme are as follows:

- It is applicable to unfair dismissal claims only.
- There must be no question relating to jurisdiction, only whether dismissal is fair or not.
- Both parties must agree to arbitration via an agreement reached with the assistance of an ACAS conciliator or a compromise agreement.
- The arbitrator will have the power to award compensation within the same limits as the tribunal, as well as re-engagement or re-instatement.
- The procedure will be non-legalistic, informal and inquisitorial rather than adversarial.
- There will be no appeal, except in very limited circumstances.
- Proceedings will be entirely private and decisions will not be published.

See Chapter 4 for further details of the various roles played by ACAS officers in dispute resolution and the potential for using external facilitators as part of the internal procedure, ie prior to employment tribunal claims.

Data Protection Act 1998

The Data Protection Act (DPA) 1998 has implications for disciplinary procedures in respect of record-keeping. Records must be relevant, accurate and secure. The ACAS Code[1] states:

> Records should be kept detailing the nature of any breach of disciplinary rules or unsatisfactory performance, the worker's defence or mitigation, the action taken and the reasons for it, whether an appeal was lodged, its outcome and any subsequent developments. These records should be kept confidential and retained in accordance with the disciplinary procedure and the Data Protection Act 1998, which requires the release of certain data to individuals on their request. Copies of any meeting records should be given to the individual concerned although in certain circumstances some information may be withheld, for example to protect a witness.

Contrary to popular belief, it is not necessary for employers to remove 'spent' disciplinary warnings from personal files. It is essential, however, to disregard their contents for disciplinary purposes after the expiry date.

Equal opportunities legislation

The ACAS Code[2] states:

> When operating disciplinary procedures, employers
> should be particularly careful not to discriminate on
> the grounds of race, gender or disability, eg whilst it
> is not unlawful to take disciplinary action against a
> pregnant woman for some reason unconnected with
> her pregnancy, it is unlawful sex discrimination and
> automatically unfair to dismiss a woman on the
> grounds of her pregnancy.

Employers also need to be aware of the dangers of infring-
ing the Disability Discrimination Act 1995 when considering ill-heath dismissals. The following case study gives a
good example of how employers can respond positively to
the health problems of employees that are likely to affect
their capability for particular work.

Case study 2 – employers must take care not to discriminate
in operating disciplinary or capability procedures
A manager working for a distribution company was concerned
when he learned that one of the HGV drivers was suffering from
a congenital condition that would, over time, lead to him being
seriously visually impaired. The manager realised that in due
course, in the absence of any reasonable adjustments that could
be made to enable the employee to carry on driving, he would
have to consider dismissing the employee. Instead he decided to
do his utmost to find suitable alternative employment within
the company. After consulting with the employee, gathering
medical evidence and seeking other specialist advice, the

manager found that he could purchase a £2,000 piece of equipment that enabled the employee to undertake the full range of duties of a warehouse operator. The employee is still working for the company.

Lessons from case law

Lesson 1

The importance of procedural safeguards has been highlighted in several leading cases, most notably in *Polkey* v *A E Dayton Services* [1987] IRLR 503. Employers will have difficulty in persuading tribunals that they have acted reasonably if they have not followed a fair procedure in dismissing an employee. The implication is that they should adhere to their own company procedure or, in its absence, the guidelines set out in the ACAS Code.

Lesson 2

Failure to permit an employee to exercise his or her right of appeal may render an otherwise fair dismissal unfair. This was established in leading cases such as *West Midlands Co-operative Society Ltd* v *Tipton* [1986] ICR 192 and *Knight* v *King Edward VI Grammar School* [1998] EAT 963.

Lesson 3

An appeal hearing can, conversely, remedy defects in a faulty disciplinary procedure – if it is sufficiently comprehensive to cure the previous deficiencies. Leading cases here include *Whitbread & Co* v *Mills* [1988] ICR 776 and *Clark* v *Civil Aviation Authority* [1991] IRLR 412.

Lesson 4

Even before the statutory right of accompaniment, case law determined that any failure by an employer to allow an employee charged with misconduct to be accompanied at a disciplinary hearing could, of itself, make the subsequent dismissal unfair. See *Willetts* v *Quick Group plc* [1992] EAT 305.

Lesson 5

Failure to follow a contractual disciplinary procedure can lead to employees with less than one year's service claiming damages for breach of contract and the loss of an opportunity to claim for unfair dismissal. See *Raspin* v *United News Shops Ltd* [1999] IRLR 9 EAT.

References

1 ACAS. *Code of Practice 1: Disciplinary and Grievance Procedures*. Clause 32. London, ACAS, 2000.
2 *Ibid*, Clause 17.

4

What should a disciplinary procedure contain?

- ✔ Main principles
- ✔ Disciplinary rules
- ✔ Gross misconduct
- ✔ Disciplinary procedures
- ✔ Contents
    - Policy statement
    - Scope
    - Types of disciplinary action
    - Levels of management authority
    - Time limits for action
    - Keeping records
    - The need for investigation/suspension with pay
    - Hearings and appeals
    - Right of accompaniment
- ✔ Sample clauses
    - Recommended clauses
    - Optional clauses
- ✔ Suggested appendices
- ✔ Small organisations
- ✔ Alternative actions

☑ Roles played by ACAS officials and other third parties
☑ References

Main principles

We shall start by proposing four main principles that should underlie your disciplinary procedure:

1 Discipline focuses on correction not punishment.
2 Disciplinary rules and procedures should be well publicised and be seen to be fair by employees.
3 Good management requires that managers seek to learn from disciplinary incidents, particularly dismissals, and will look at what can be done to avoid repetitions.
4 Regardless of how well designed disciplinary policies and procedures are, it is the handling of disciplinary incidents that is the key to success. Managers must therefore be well trained and confident in their roles.

Disciplinary rules

Disciplinary rules set the standards of behaviour and conduct expected in the workplace. The contents of the rules vary greatly, depending on the size and location of the organisation, the industry, type of work, working conditions and history of employee relations. Yet they generally make reference to the following:

- general conduct
- health and safety

- security
- time-keeping and attendance
- use of company facilities
- discrimination.

It is unlikely that the rules will be contained in one document or that they can cover all the circumstances that arise. They will emanate from a number of sources, including:

- the statement of terms and conditions
- the staff handbook
- organisational rules
- company policies and procedures, eg health and safety
- codes of conduct
- company intranet sites
- information on performance standards
- custom and practice.

In the words of Martin and Jackson:[1]

> Disciplinary rules help to ensure a consistent and fair approach to the treatment of employees. Managers obviously wish to have a disciplined workforce, but the majority of employees are likely to be just as keen to have a set of rules in operation so that their working lives can be reasonably orderly. Also, employees want to know what the rules are in order to determine what they should be doing (or not be doing) in order to be successful within the organisation.

In essence, rules must be:

- clear and unambiguous

- relevant to the workers concerned
- consistently applied
- accessible to all (including disabled workers and those for whom English is not their first language)
- up to date, eg legislative constraints concerning working hours and holidays should be included as well as the effect of technological advances such as increased access to the Internet.

Case study 3 – disciplinary rules must be relevant and up to date

A local authority recently saw a disciplinary decision overturned on appeal. A temporary clerical assistant had been issued with a written warning by her manager because she refused to comply with the council's dress code which prohibited visible body piercings, except for one earring per ear. The appeals panel were sympathetic to the employee's argument that this rule was outdated and inappropriate to the majority of council employees, ie those who did not have direct dealings with the council's clients. The written warning was withdrawn and the dress code is currently being revised in the light of the case, equal opportunities in general and the Human Rights Act 1998.

Gross misconduct

Not all misconduct is of the same severity and minor breaches should receive lesser penalties. How will employees know which actions are likely to lead to their dismissal? It is sensible, within disciplinary procedures, to provide a non-exhaustive list of offences that will normally be regarded as examples of gross misconduct, justifying summary dismissal. Summary dismissal is dismissal without notice or pay in lieu of notice and is justifiable only where the employee's action is felt to be so serious that it goes to the root of the employment relationship.

Common examples would include theft, fraud, serious health and safety infringements, fighting, assault, bullying, harassment, discrimination, serious negligence, disloyalty, insubordination or serious breaches of company policies such as those on smoking, drugs or alcohol in the workplace. In any event, proper investigation is the key to a successful summary dismissal, as is illustrated in the case study below.

> **Case study 4 – a thorough investigation is necessary, especially in potential gross misconduct cases**
>
> An Internet insurance company was informed that one of its call centre staff had given bad advice to a customer, which would have resulted in his motor insurance policy being void. It was alleged that he had suggested that the customer's common law wife could benefit from a discount that was only applicable to spouses. The company took pains to carry out a full investigation before presenting the employee with all the evidence. As a result, although he was given ample opportunity to state his side of the case, he quickly decided to resign, fully aware that he had committed an act of gross misconduct.

Disciplinary procedures

Disciplinary procedures provide guidelines for adherence to the rules and a fair method of dealing with infringements. The ACAS Code[2] lists the essential features of disciplinary procedures (the bracketed comments in italics are explanatory). Disciplinary procedures should:

i) be in writing

ii) specify to whom they apply *(there may be different procedures for different groups of employees, eg salaried staff and hourly paid employees)*

iii) be non-discriminatory *(ie in line with statutory provisions as well as not allowing managers to use disciplinary procedures to victimise or make examples of certain employees)*

iv) provide for matters to be dealt with without undue delay *(subject to a thorough investigation)*

v) provide for proceedings, witness statements and records to be kept confidential *(see the section on the DPA 1998 in Chapter 3)*

vi) indicate the disciplinary actions which may be taken *(see below)*

vii) specify the levels of management which have the authority to take the various forms of disciplinary action *(see below)*

viii) provide for workers to be informed of the complaints against them and, where possible, all relevant evidence before any hearing

ix) provide workers with an opportunity to state their case before decisions are reached *(even employees apparently 'caught in the act' should never be instantly dismissed without a proper disciplinary hearing)*

x) provide workers with the right to be accompanied *(see Chapter 3)*

xi) ensure that, except for gross misconduct, no worker is dismissed for a first breach of discipline

xii) ensure that disciplinary action is not taken until the case has been carefully investigated

xiii) ensure that workers are given an explanation for any penalty imposed *(ie the reason for the decision, the length of time for which the disciplinary action will remain on their personal record and the consequences of future breaches of the disciplinary rules)*

xiv) provide a right of appeal – normally to a more senior manager – and specify the procedure to be followed.

Contents

So what should your disciplinary procedure contain? The following headings are suggested.

Policy statement

Organisations often introduce their disciplinary procedure with a statement of policy. This sets out the purpose of the procedure. A typical statement reads as follows:

> In order to meet our business objectives, the company expects all its employees to attain acceptable standards of work performance, behaviour and attendance at all times. We are committed to supporting and encouraging our employees in achieving this. The disciplinary procedure is intended

to make sure that these standards are maintained in a fair, consistent and systematic way.

Scope

Who does the disciplinary procedure cover? This will obviously vary depending on the organisational circumstances.

Example 1

This disciplinary procedure applies to all members of staff subject to the following provisos:

a) if you have less than one year's service, the disciplinary procedure may not be applied in full

b) if you are a senior manager, you will be asked to attain standards of performance and conduct in shorter timescales.

Example 2

This disciplinary procedure applies to all employees except:

a) the chief executive

b) those terminated on grounds of redundancy

c) those still on a probationary period.

Separate procedures apply in these cases.

Types of disciplinary action

Breaches of disciplinary rules vary in their seriousness but you are not obliged to work your way through the hierarchical system of warnings. You may issue any sanctions you deem to be appropriate (see the table on page 36 for an example). Thus, in general:

- Minor infringements might merit a formal or informal oral warning (recorded or unrecorded) – eg an occasional late arrival at work.
- More serious infringements might result in a written warning – eg failure to complete quality checks properly.
- Gross misconduct will probably result in summary dismissal – eg theft of company property.

You should take into account the following points:

1 The intention of the informal warning stage is to give the employee a chance to put things right before anything goes on record. Thus problems can be 'nipped in the bud', hopefully averting the need for any formal action.

2 There are a number of other possible actions short of dismissal that you may wish to include in your new procedure. These include disciplinary transfers, suspension without pay, demotion, loss of seniority, loss of increments and fines, but these penalties cannot be used on an ad hoc basis and must have been allowed for in the contract of employment.

3 You may also decide to withdraw privileges, as a result of disciplinary investigations, if you feel they are being abused, eg flexitime, company sick pay. Company schemes need to be carefully drafted to allow for this.

Levels of management authority

Here we are concerned with who is authorised to take the initial disciplinary decision and who must hear the appeal (see the table on page 36 for an example). The importance of getting this right is demonstrated by the following case study.

> **Case study 5 – ensure that it is the manager who is authorised to do so who makes the decision on disciplinary action**
>
> In a stockbroking environment, the general atmosphere was one where political correctness was ridiculed and laddish behaviour was encouraged. A departmental manager discovered that one of his team had downloaded racist materials from the Internet and was appalled when he realised that the materials incited criminal behaviour; in his view, this behaviour justified summary dismissal. In the company procedure the manager was authorised to take disciplinary action up to and including dismissal. During the investigation, the employee admitted that he was the guilty party. The manager appeared to have an open and shut case but made the mistake of seeking permission from his boss to effect the dismissal. This was contrary to natural justice and also threatened the impartiality of the appeals process, since it should have been the boss who would hear the appeal. In this particular case, the manager was lucky, in that the employee went quietly and did not challenge the disciplinary decision by making an internal appeal or tribunal claim.

Time limits for action

Another consideration of natural justice is that there should be a time limit beyond which a disciplinary action should be disregarded by the employer. Generally organisations set time limits of between three and 12 months, which tend to vary according to the level of disciplinary action (see the table on page 36 for an example).

Keeping records

We have already stated that you must ensure that adequate records of disciplinary offences are kept. See the table on page 36 for examples of the records that would be applicable at different levels of disciplinary action.

The need for investigation/suspension with pay

The ACAS Code[3] states that:

> When a disciplinary matter arises, the relevant supervisor or manager should first establish the facts promptly before recollections fade and, where appropriate, obtain statements from any available witnesses.

It would be wise, however, to ensure that the investigation is carried out by someone other than the manager conducting the disciplinary interview. Further, in cases of suspected gross misconduct, it is generally advisable, though not a foregone conclusion, to suspend the employee concerned on full pay during such investigations. This action will be most relevant where relationships have broken down or where there are risks to the company's property or other parties. It should be made clear to the employee that the suspension is not a punishment in itself.

Hearings and appeals

These two crucial parts of the disciplinary procedure are dealt with in more detail in Chapter 6 when we consider how to make disciplinary procedures work. In the meantime, you should note that some organisations have appeals mechanisms that encompass more than one stage. There may be good reasons for this but often they are only there

A template disciplinary procedure

Type of offence	Disciplinary action	Action taken by:	Appeal to:	Time limit before action disregarded	Records kept
Minor breaches of rules and standards	Informal oral warning	Immediate supervisor	Line manager senior to supervisor	N/A	Diary note by supervisor
Repetition of minor breaches	Formal oral warning	Immediate supervisor	Line manager senior to supervisor	6 months	*Written confirmation to employee, copied to the personal file with relevant evidence. Notes of meetings, including any investigations (copied to the employee). Note on disciplinary record
Repetition of minor breaches, or a more serious breach	Written warning	Line manager	Senior manager	9 months	ditto
Failure to improve after written warning, or a very serious breach	Final written warning	Line manager	Senior manager	12 months	ditto
Failure to improve after final written warning or gross misconduct	Dismissal or action short of dismissal	Senior manager	Director	12 months for action short of dismissal	ditto

* This will include confirmation, where applicable, of the penalty and reasons for it, plan of action, time limits, consequences of repetition and right of appeal.

because of historical factors and can lead to a protracted process. In any event, procedures should specify that managers hearing appeals are not those who conducted the investigation or disciplinary interview and, preferably, are more senior. They should also specify the procedure for submitting an appeal, eg it should be in writing to the personnel department, and the timescale for doing so.

Right of accompaniment

The new statutory right of accompaniment applies to unionised and non-unionised environments. Many organisations already allow employees to be accompanied to formal disciplinary hearings, sometimes even allowing outside parties such as solicitors or family members to attend. If you have not already done so, you should review this to see whether it fully complies with the provisions of the ERA 1999, backed up by the ACAS Code.

You should by now have a good idea about what needs to be included in your new or revised disciplinary procedure. Some sample clauses are provided below to assist you further.

Sample clauses

All organisations must ensure that their disciplinary procedures are not only up to date but also tailored to their own circumstances. Below we list some suggestions, which can be adapted, for inclusion in your disciplinary procedure.

Recommended clauses

Appendix 1 contains Barbour Index's sample disciplinary policy, principles and procedure (which includes reference to a separate capability procedure). The notes to the same policy include many useful clauses other employers may want to incorporate, perhaps in adapted form, into their own procedures:

- This procedure is for guidance only and does not form part of employees' contractual rights. The contents may be subject to revision from time to time.
- A second management representative from another function may be invited to attend formal disciplinary meetings in order to act as a witness and note-taker.
- The timescales listed above will be adhered to wherever possible. However, where there are good reasons, eg the need for further investigation or the lack of availability of witnesses or companions, each party can request that the other agrees to an extension of the permitted timescale.
- The company reserves the right to seek assistance from external facilitators at any stage in the disciplinary procedure, in the interests of seeking a satisfactory outcome for all those concerned.
- For employees during their first year of employment, the company reserves the right to speed up the decision-making process and therefore may choose to follow a truncated version of the above procedure.
- The grievance procedure should not be used for appeals against disciplinary decisions, as that is the purpose of the disciplinary appeals procedure. If, however, you have a complaint against the

behaviour of a manager during the course of a disciplinary case, you may raise it as a grievance with a senior manager. If necessary, the disciplinary procedure may be suspended for a short period until the grievance can be considered. Further, another manager may be brought in to deal with the disciplinary case.

Other recommended clauses include:

- The list of gross misconduct examples above is not intended to be exhaustive and the examples are given for illustrative purposes only.
- If it is considered that a more detailed investigation is required, then a formal investigation will be undertaken prior to any decision to convene a disciplinary hearing. This investigation should normally be completed within 28 days.
- Where it is not possible or appropriate for the manager authorised in the disciplinary procedure to conduct the disciplinary hearing or appeal, a nominated deputy will be appointed.
- At the conclusion of the appeal hearing, the manager or director involved may reduce or increase the original disciplinary penalty. The decision of the manager or director hearing the appeal shall be final.
- Where an appeal against a dismissal fails, the effective date of termination is the date on which the employee was originally dismissed, not the date when the employee was told that his or her appeal had failed. Where an appeal against

dismissal succeeds, the employee will be paid any monies due for the intervening period and continuity of service will be preserved.

Optional clauses

- Disciplinary action will be taken against a union representative only after the full circumstances of the case have been discussed with a full-time official of the appropriate trade union.
- It is unlikely that a warning that has expired will be referred to again in any further disciplinary action. However, if a pattern of behaviour emerges or an act of misconduct is repeated, the company will take account of previous related offences.
- Observers will not be allowed to attend any stage of the disciplinary process except for training purposes.
- The procedure will apply to all employees, including probationary, temporary and seasonal employees. Employees who are on fixed-term or short-term contracts will not have their contracts extended solely for the purpose of completing disciplinary proceedings.

Suggested appendices

You may also wish to consider providing further information as appendices to your procedure, for example:
- flowcharts to represent the decision-making process
- model investigation report forms

- standard letters inviting employees to take part in investigations/disciplinary hearings/appeals and to confirm the outcome of disciplinary proceedings
- guidelines for conducting disciplinary hearings and appeals
- a checklist for taking notes of the meetings (see *Appendix 2* for an example).

Small organisations

Employment tribunals are required to consider questions of reasonableness in unfair dismissal claims in accordance with the size and administrative resources of the employers concerned. Further, it is generally accepted that small organisations, ie those with fewer than 20 employees, cannot be expected to have sophisticated procedures in place. However, recent research suggests that small employers are disproportionately represented in unfair dismissal claims and have a lower success rate in defending them than larger establishments. This is often because they are more likely to be guilty of procedural failings.

What is the solution? Issues of poor performance or conduct can be even more disruptive in small organisations and it is therefore worth investing time and money into tackling them. We strongly recommend that small organisations have written rules and procedures in place that incorporate the ACAS 'essential features' listed above, and that they ensure managers are trained in handling discipline.

A further problem for small companies concerns the employee's right of appeal. For instance, the managing director may be the only person authorised to dispense disciplinary sanctions and would therefore have difficulty in being impartial at an appeals hearing. One option is the use of third parties, eg independent arbitration, as the appeals stage of an internal procedure (see below). Chapter 9 refers to further sources of information specifically aimed at small employers.

Alternative actions

We have already stressed the importance of good day-to-day management practices such as informal oral warnings in helping to avert the need for disciplinary sanctions. Often, even when disciplinary breaches have occurred, neither formal nor informal disciplinary action is considered to be appropriate. This could be because the employee's personal circumstances mitigate in his or her favour, eg recent latenesses may be explained by a change in domestic circumstances. In such cases, managers may decide that informal advice, coaching or counselling would be more successful strategies. Sometimes 'cutting the employee some slack', eg making temporary changes to working hours or job content, can be particularly beneficial as the employer is visibly supporting the employee during a difficult time.

The chart opposite (adapted from Martin and Jackson[4]) sets out the decision-making process and provides a link to our next chapter on capability procedures.

Roles played by ACAS officials and other third parties

The mission of the Advisory, Conciliation and Arbitration Service (ACAS) is (*cont.* p 44):

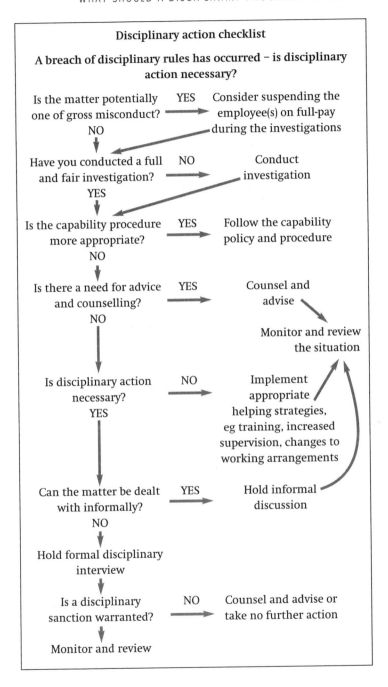

Disciplinary action checklist

A breach of disciplinary rules has occurred – is disciplinary action necessary?

Is the matter potentially one of gross misconduct? — YES → Consider suspending the employee(s) on full-pay during the investigations

NO ↓

Have you conducted a full and fair investigation? — NO → Conduct investigation

YES ↓

Is the capability procedure more appropriate? — YES → Follow the capability policy and procedure

NO ↓

Is there a need for advice and counselling? — YES → Counsel and advise ↘ Monitor and review the situation

NO ↓

Is disciplinary action necessary? — NO → Implement appropriate helping strategies, eg training, increased supervision, changes to working arrangements

YES ↓

Can the matter be dealt with informally? — YES → Hold informal discussion

NO ↓

Hold formal disciplinary interview ↓

Is a disciplinary sanction warranted? — NO → Counsel and advise or take no further action

↓

Monitor and review

> To improve the performance and effectiveness of organisations by providing an independent and impartial service to prevent and resolve disputes and to build harmonious relationships at work.

ACAS activities include giving advice, voluntary conciliation, mediation and arbitration.

With regard to discipline, ACAS officers would be unlikely to play a role while internal procedures are still in operation, though their network of public enquiry points will provide free advice to individuals and organisations involved in pursuing or responding to disciplinary incidents. The picture changes when the employment relationship has come to an end and ACAS has a statutory duty to conciliate in actual and potential unfair dismissal and breach-of-contract claims to employment tribunals. The aim is to resolve the matter before it gets to a tribunal via a settlement, withdrawal of the claim or an alternative solution such as reinstatement.

Trade unions also have a lot of experience in disciplinary matters They clearly have a role to play in representing or accompanying employees to formal hearings but also, in common with management, have an interest in promoting standards of conduct within the workplace. Further, if your organisation is unionised, you will need the support and agreement of the trade union(s) before finalising a new or revised disciplinary procedure.

What about other third parties? In one of the recommended clauses above, the option of providing a role for external facilitators in your disciplinary procedure was mooted. Third parties can include ACAS officials and ACAS-appointed or -recommended independent mediators or arbitrators, plus other qualified mediators, lawyers, members of the council (for local authorities), advice centre workers, union officials or other persons deemed to be suitably experienced and impartial. More and more organisations are finding that third-party intervention is particularly powerful in resolving disciplinary disputes.

Further, Citizens' Advice Bureaux (CAB) have extensive experience in advising individuals about their employment rights. CAB staff also provide advice to employers and, given adequate resources, may be willing to play a facilitating role in internal disciplinary procedures. Finally, if discrimination is involved, bodies such as the Commission for Racial Equality, Equal Opportunities Commission and the Disability Rights Commission may be called upon as another source of help and advice.

References

1 MARTIN M. and JACKSON T. Personnel Practice. 2nd edn, London, Chartered Institute of Personnel and Development, 2000, p102.
2 ACAS. Code of Practice 1: Disciplinary and Grievance Procedures. Clause 9. London, ACAS, 2000.
3 Ibid, Clause 11.
4 MARTIN M. and JACKSON T. op cit, p107.

5

What should a capability procedure contain?

☑ Introduction
☑ Poor performance
☑ Ill-health
☑ Contents and sample clauses
    Policy statement
    Scope
    Distinction between disciplinary and capability cases
    Distinction between long-term and short-term sickness absences
    Investigation
    Medical investigation
    Expected standard of performance
    Procedural steps
    Hearings and appeals
    Warnings and a chance to improve
    Support mechanisms
    Review periods
    Alternative employment
    Possible alternative actions
    Disabled employees
    Right of accompaniment

☑ Other recommended clauses
☑ Optional clauses
☑ Suggested appendices
☑ Conclusion
☑ References

Introduction

It is not our intention here to provide a comprehensive account of capability procedures (which could be the subject matter for another book). Instead, we shall be giving concise guidance on the differences between disciplinary and capability procedures and the essential features of the latter.

Most managers would agree that dealing with poor performance is one of their most difficult responsibilities. The problems are summed up in the following quote from an Industrial Relations Law Bulletin:[1]

> Incompetent or negligent work has possible adverse repercussions on productivity and efficiency, health and safety, and customer or client relations, as well as the morale and performance of the organisation's other employees. Consequently, no organisation seeking to compete effectively can afford to ignore the problem in the hope that things might improve by themselves. On the other hand, applying a heavy-handed approach that brings the full force of disciplinary procedures to bear upon the under-performing individual may ultimately expose the employer to claims under statutory employment

protection laws, in particular those governing unfair dismissal.

We have already said that poor performance may be a conduct or a capability issue and that investigations are therefore necessary to determine which route is the appropriate one. In general:

- If the reason for the poor performance lies within the employee's control – eg negligence, lack of application or an attitudinal problem – the disciplinary procedure applies.
- If the reason lies outside the employee's control – eg health, lack of skills or qualifications, the changing nature of the job, personal circumstances – the capability procedure applies.

Do you need separate procedures to deal with ill-heath and poor performance that is not health related? There are some differences between the steps that need to be taken, but also many similarities, so it is up to you to choose what your capability procedure will cover. In *Appendix 3* we provide an example of a capability procedure that covers poor performance due to a genuine lack of capability but not sickness absence problems, which are dealt with elsewhere.

Poor performance

Capability problems can, for the most part, be prevented by recruiting the right people in the first place. By the 'right people' we mean those who possess the requisite knowledge and skills and, after appropriate training, can produce work of good quality in accordance with sensible deadlines.

Poor performance may occur, however, for a variety of reasons and the emphasis in dealing with it should be on open and honest communications, backed up by support mechanisms that assist the employee in reaching the required standards of performance.

An important message from unfair dismissal case law is that employers must have a reasonable belief that the employee is incompetent or unsuitable for the job and must have followed a fair procedure. ACAS[2] suggests that employers follow the framework below:

- the employee should be asked for an explanation, and the explanation checked
- where the reason is a lack of the required skills, the employee should, wherever practicable, be assisted through training and given reasonable time to reach the required standard of performance
- where despite encouragement and assistance the employee is unable to reach the required standard of performance, consideration should be given to finding suitable alternative work
- where alternative work is not available, the position should be explained to the employee before dismissal action is taken
- an employee should not normally be dismissed because of poor performance unless warnings and a chance to improve have been given *(exceptions would include a case of negligence that had serious safety consequences)*
- if the main cause of poor performance is the changing nature of the job, employers should

consider whether the situation may properly be treated as a redundancy matter rather than a capability or conduct issue.

Ill-health

The key elements of an ill-health capability procedure are:

- consultation with the employee, ie maintaining regular contacts throughout the period of absence and fully involving the employee in the decision-making process
- medical investigation, ie gathering medical evidence and an indication of the likelihood of an early return to work and the suitability of the current position
- consideration, where appropriate, of alternative employment (and/or reasonable adjustments in the case of disabled employees) before any decision to dismiss the employee.

Following the above good practice guidelines should stand you in good stead in internal appeals and employment tribunal cases, but unfortunately there are many pitfalls in store for you in ill-health dismissals. What if the dismissal occurred during the employee's contractual entitlement to sick pay? In such a case, the employee may have a claim for breach of contract if there is no express term to permit this. You should note the following three-stage approach to dismissing an employee on the grounds of sickness:

1 Check the contract of employment for relevant clauses and seek legal advice if there are ambiguities.

2 Ensure that you follow a correct procedure (see the key elements listed above).

3 Ensure that the provisions of the Disability Discrimination Act (DDA) 1995 are taken into account before making your final decision. See *Case study 6* for an example of a good practice approach to handling an ill-health case.

Case study 6 – follow good practice in capability cases

A newly appointed personnel manager was asked by a department manager whether she could dismiss an employee for poor performance. The personnel manager investigated the case and discovered that the employee was unaware that her performance was unsatisfactory because the manager had not instigated a formal capability procedure. The employee had medical problems that stemmed from a period of post-natal depression, but she now had an underlying psychological condition for which she was awaiting treatment. The company had temporarily reduced her hours to accommodate her difficulties, but her sickness absence record was still well above average. Further, when she was at work, her behaviour was disruptive to the rest of the team. The personnel manager gathered more medical evidence about the employee's condition and was informed that she would have to wait for several months for treatment if she was reliant on the NHS. The employee was consulted throughout the process and was made aware of the company's concerns. She accepted their offer to pay for therapy, which she is currently undergoing. The early indications are that she will make a full recovery and return to work in due course.

Contents and sample clauses

So what should your capability procedure contain? In our suggestions below, we are assuming that your procedure will cover ill-health and other poor performance cases. As always, the sample clauses will need to be tailored to your organisational circumstances.

Policy statement

The company will at all times endeavour to ensure that employees achieve and maintain a high standard of performance in their work. To this end the company will ensure that standards are established, performance is monitored and employees are given appropriate training and support to meet these standards.

Scope

This capability procedure applies to all employees but, if you are serving your probationary period, the capability procedure may not be applied in full.

Distinction between disciplinary and capability cases

In dealing with cases of poor performance, the company distinguishes between those where the cause is within the employee's control, eg negligence, lack of application or attitudinal problems, and those where it is outside the employee's control, eg health, lack of training or the changing nature of the job. In the former case, the company's disciplinary procedure will be used and, in the latter, the capability procedure.

Distinction between long-term and short-term sickness absences

This clause should state whether the procedure differs when sickness absences are short term or long term.

The following procedure will be operated where your immediate manager establishes that:

- *your attendance record is significantly worse than those of comparable employees or creates a particular operational difficulty (refer to the section on short-term absences below), or*
- *your absence due to sickness has gone on for a considerable length of time (refer to the section on long-term absences below).*

Investigation

This clause should set out what evidence will be collected, and how, in order to establish the reason/s for poor performance.

Medical investigation

The interview will seek to establish the reasons for your absence and its likely duration. You may be requested to allow the company to contact your GP in order to establish the likely length of absence and the long-term effect on your capability in relation to job performance and attendance at work. You may also be required to attend an examination by a medical practitioner of the company's choice.

Expected standard of performance

During the discussions you will be afforded the opportunity to ask questions regarding the standard of performance expected of you.

Procedural steps

This clause should cover reference to the informal and formal stages, including the right of appeal.

Hearings and appeals

This clause should cover how these will be conducted and which manager/s are involved at each stage.

Warnings and a chance to improve

This clause should make clear that managers should reiterate what is expected of the employee, how the performance currently falls short of the standard, the timescale for achieving the standard and the consequences of a failure to do so.

Support mechanisms

This clause should make reference to the provision of counselling, training, additional supervision, frequent monitoring, etc.

Review periods

This clause should set these out in light of the following factors:

- the employee's length of service
- the quality of performance during that service
- how far below standard the performance has fallen
- for how long the problem was left unattended.

Alternative employment

If there has been no discernible improvement, your manager will explain to you that you have failed to improve. Consideration will be given to whether there are alternative vacancies that you would be competent to fill. If there are, you will be given the option of accepting such a vacancy or being dismissed.

Possible alternative actions

This clause should set out sanctions such as no salary review, demotion or dismissal.

Disabled employees

The company will consider making reasonable adjustments to your job to accommodate your short-term or long-term requirements if you are considered to be disabled within the meaning of the DDA 1995.

Right of accompaniment

At all formal meetings, you will have the right to be accompanied by a colleague, lay or trade union official.

Other recommended clauses

- *This procedure is for guidance only and does not form part of employees' contractual rights. The contents may be subject to revision from time to time.*
- *A second management representative from another function may be invited to attend formal capability meetings in order to act as a witness and note-taker.*
- *The company reserves the right to seek assistance from external facilitators at any stage in the capability procedure, in the interests of seeking a satisfactory outcome for all those concerned.*
- *For employees during their first year of employment, the company reserves the right to speed up the decision-making process and therefore may choose to follow a truncated version of the above procedure.*
- *Where it is not possible or appropriate for the manager authorised in the capability procedure to conduct the*

hearing or appeal, a nominated deputy will be appointed.

- *Appeal against management decisions will be heard in accordance with the company's disciplinary appeals procedure.*

Optional clauses

- *The company will take a decision to dismiss at a time that is appropriate to the individual circumstances of the case. This is in no way governed by whether or not the employee concerned has exhausted his or her sick pay entitlement.*
- *Probationary employees or those on fixed-term or short-term contracts will not have their contracts extended solely for the purpose of completing capability proceedings.*
- *At any stage in this procedure, if your manager (following investigations) feels that your absences are not due to an underlying medical condition but are casual in nature, the company's disciplinary procedure will be invoked.*

Suggested appendices

See Chapter 4.

Conclusion

The more steps you take to assist employees in improving their performance, the more likely that you will succeed in defending an unfair dismissal claim. The main pitfalls to avoid are:

- not taking action early enough
- being inconsistent, eg awarding a salary increase to an employee who has a warning on file
- letting review periods overrun
- neither offering nor responding to requests for appropriate support mechanisms
- not following the procedural steps.

References

1 IRS. 'Capability and qualifications'. *IRS Employment Review: Industrial Relations Law Bulletin 610*. February 1999. p7.
2 ACAS. *Discipline at Work*. Advisory Handbook. S.10, London, ACAS, Revised November 2000.

How do we make our procedure work?

☑	Introduction
☑	Design and implementation
☑	Audit existing arrangements
☑	Consult the workforce
☑	Pilot the procedure
☑	Publicise the procedure
☑	Provide training and guidance
☑	Revise associated documentation
☑	Integrate with other management activities
☑	Operation
☑	Monitoring and evaluation
☑	Reference

Introduction

This chapter deals with the practicalities of operating a disciplinary procedure. The skills and knowledge aspects are covered in Chapter 7. These guidelines should apply equally to the operation of capability procedures but, as before, we shall use the term disciplinary procedure to cover both.

We start with some guidance on how to ensure the successful design and implementation of your new (or revised) disciplinary procedure. We then highlight some good practice tips on operating your procedure. Finally we stress the need to monitor and evaluate success.

Design and implementation

Chapters 4 and 5 covered the possible contents of your procedures. In designing your procedure, you should ensure that it:

- reflects the legislative requirements
- is suited to your organisational circumstances
- is workable.

We shall follow the seven main stages of design and implementation recommended in the companion book by Tricia Jackson[1] on handling grievances. They are as follows:

1 Audit the existing arrangements.
2 Consult the workforce.
3 Pilot the new procedure.
4 Publicise the procedure.
5 Provide training and guidance.
6 Revise associated documentation.
7 Integrate the procedure with other management activities.

Audit existing arrangements

We recommend that a working party is established at the beginning of this process to undertake the range of necessary tasks. Its members should be drawn from all sectors and levels of the workforce and, where applicable, should include trade union representatives.

The working party will need to use a number of auditing tools such as checking records, carrying out interviews and benchmarking against other organisations as well as to become familiar with legislative requirements. Looking at the recent past, they will be seeking to answer the following questions:

- Does the existing procedure (written or unwritten) comply with current legislation?
- How accurate are existing records on disciplinary incidents?
- How easy is it to analyse these data?
- What are the views of managers and workers on the content and structure of the existing arrangements?
- Are these arrangements user-friendly?
- Is there currently a distinction between the handling of conduct and capability issues?
- What are the main reasons for disciplinary action?
- In which departments/areas are they prevalent?
- What percentage of disciplinary actions result in appeals, and what are the results?
- How many cases have resulted in dismissals?
- How many gross misconduct cases have occurred?
- How many employment tribunal claims have been related to discipline and dismissal, and what have been the outcomes?
- What other options, such as the use of external parties, could be considered for inclusion in the new procedure?

- What changes in working practices, communications and written policies have arisen as a result of disciplinary cases?
- What are the links between disciplinary and capability procedures and other management activities such as performance appraisal?
- How often are compromise agreements used in potential disputes?
- Does the use of compromise agreements reflect management indecision in handling conduct or capability issues?

Consult the workforce

It is important to have in place disciplinary rules and procedures that employees view as fair and reasonable. We therefore recommend that you seek views and suggestions from as wide a spectrum of the workforce as possible before finalising the design and content of the new procedure. Managers' views are also important here as they will have the role of implementing the procedure and therefore need to be convinced that it will work. This consultation can often be done via existing mechanisms such as team meetings, newsletters, the intranet, questionnaires, etc.

In a unionised environment, union representatives will be the obvious parties to consult, and their approval may be necessary in the latter stages as the disciplinary procedure may become a procedural agreement. In other organisations, consultation is equally important since the disciplinary procedure will impose new obligations on employees and their consent is therefore necessary.

Pilot the procedure

This may seem to be a strange suggestion in the light of the subject matter of this book, but it is important to ensure that the new procedure is easy to understand and not open to misinterpretation. For instance, the levels of management authority may not be clear because the term 'immediate supervisor' has been used when, in some departments, team leaders and supervisors are employed. Alternatively, the operation of the appeals mechanism may not have been clearly set out, resulting in uncertainty about whether the manager who meted out the disciplinary sanction should be in attendance. If the manager does not attend, then when is his or her side of the case heard?

How can you pilot the new procedure? This can be achieved either by working through a number of hypothetical situations (this could be combined with management training) or by carrying out trial runs on actual cases (with the permission of those involved).

The final procedure, as amended, must then be approved by senior managers and agreed with other appropriate parties before being publicised.

Publicise the procedure

It is essential for all employees and managers to be made aware of the new procedure. Employment tribunal cases have been lost on the grounds that organisations could not provide enough evidence to back up their claims that employees were familiar with their disciplinary rules and procedures.

There are a number of options available to you:

- Announce its introduction, aims and contents with a letter from the managing director or chief executive.
- Introduce the new procedure by carrying out a series of briefings for line managers, other key personnel and union/employee representatives.
- Display the new procedure on notice boards and/or the company intranet and issue copies to all workers.
- Reinforce the message via existing communication mechanisms such as team briefings and internal newsletters.
- Change relevant procedures and the staff handbook to reflect the new procedure.
- Include discussion of the disciplinary procedure at induction.
- Continue the process by being open about the lessons learned as a result of disciplinary incidents, eg announcing changes that have been made to written policies or management activities.

Furthermore, if management decide to 'clamp down' on certain activities, eg time-keeping, 'casual' sickness absence or private work during company time, they should publicise this by, say, including it on the agenda of team meetings or issuing e-mails to all concerned.

Provide training and guidance

This is a very important stage because, as we have already said, having a comprehensive new procedure is not enough on its own. Handling disciplinary matters is a complex business, with potentially costly results if managed badly. Managers must be trained in good practices in order to build up their confidence and competence.

You may decide to provide specific training programmes that cover the skills and knowledge required for effective disciplinary handling, including record-keeping (see Chapter 7 for more details). Alternatively, new or revised procedures may be introduced via awareness training sessions, backed up by coaching and advice from specialist staff, as and when managers require it. In some organisations personnel specialists play an active role in the formal disciplinary stages and can therefore oversee the proceedings as well as supporting less experienced line managers.

The provision of training may be extended to union and other employee representatives or companions (though generally trade unions provide their own training). Further, the personnel department should be seen as a source of advice and assistance, and guidance notes can be prepared for all parties, eg managers, representatives, companions and employees.

Revise associated documentation

A new or revised disciplinary procedure has implications for the contract of employment. On the assumption that any changes to the existing arrangements have been properly agreed, you now need to ensure that you revise all associated documentation to remove any anomalies. This includes the statement of terms and conditions, staff handbook, codes of conduct, induction information, equal opportunities policy, grievance procedure, health and safety policy, performance appraisal scheme, etc. You may also, in the process of researching this issue, have found that new or revised policies and procedures are needed in certain areas, eg on bullying and harassment, e-mail and Internet usage, alcohol and drugs, smoking, sickness absence or flexible working arrangements.

Case study 7 – disciplinary incidents may raise the need for new policies, procedures and/or working practices

The managing director at a specialist recruitment company prided herself on giving staff a big thank you at Christmas by arranging a dinner, disco and accommodation at an expensive London hotel for employees and their partners. The company paid for everything, including a free bar until the early hours of the morning. Imagine her horror last Christmas when she was presented with a bill for damages to one of her employee's bedrooms; a result, it appeared, of high spirits of a number of the younger staff. The employees were disciplined, but the MD felt that her hands were tied by the lack of specific rules on the use of alcohol and drugs and the standards of behaviour expected outside of working hours. A new alcohol and drugs policy and revised code of conduct have since been introduced and employees will be reminded about them before next year's Christmas party.

Integrate with other management activities

We have already said that employing sound management practices should help to reduce the need for disciplinary action. Thus clear rules, good communications and leading by example can all help to create a positive environment. Coupled with the effective use of informal warnings, these should mean that fewer formal warnings are necessary. You cannot, however, wave a magic wand and achieve this overnight. In the meantime, therefore, we would contend that managers must review their experiences of handling discipline and decide whether changes need to be made to other management activities to avoid a reoccurrence of the problems.

For instance, if your disciplinary rules prohibit moon-lighting by employees, incidents of this offence may indicate:

- that the rule is not relevant to lower-graded staff and should be reworded
- that staff feel that their earnings are low and that they need to supplement their incomes, in which case a review of reward packages may be necessary.

The following case study further demonstrates this point.

Case study 8 – disciplinary incidents may lead to a review of other management activities

A new recruit was appointed to the role of customer services manager in an organisation that specialises in providing information services to the engineering industry. She quickly realised there were problems with the performance of the team leader and tried, by various means, to resolve them. She was surprised to see that the previous manager had issued a number of written warnings but had, at the same time, awarded the team leader the maximum performance bonus. The new manager, despite many hours spent in discussions with the employee, was unable to motivate her enough to achieve her performance targets. Regrettably the employment relationship came to an end when a compromise agreement was breached. The manager, after reviewing this unhappy experience, decided to write a report to the chief executive suggesting the following actions:

- a review of recruitment and selection procedures, as it was doubtful that the employee should ever have been promoted to the role of team leader
- a review of the performance management system so that the above contradictions could not occur again.

Operation

We have throughout this book sought to highlight good practices in operating disciplinary procedures. The key points are summarised opposite and some of them further illustrated with case study examples.

Good practice tips
Ensure that the organisational climate and culture is a supportive one.
Employ good day-to-day management practices, eg carry out performance appraisal interviews in accordance with the timetable and ensure that current disciplinary/capability issues are taken account of.
Make special allowances for individuals who are disabled or whose first language is not English.
Follow the procedure.
Investigate fully.
Take notes of investigations and meetings and keep records.
Notify the employee of their rights.
Think through the consequences of chosen sanctions.
Apply rules consistently but flexibly, ie take into account any precedents but also mitigating circumstances (see *Case study 9* below).
Ensure follow-up action is taken, eg remove flexi-time privileges for an agreed period of time.
Reinforce disciplinary rules and publicise outcomes where appropriate (see *Case study 10* below).
Monitor the employee's progress and arrange review meetings at appropriate intervals.
Be prepared to learn from each disciplinary experience and take action, eg review inappropriate rules or working methods that lead to employee resentment.

Case study 9 – managers should take into account mitigating circumstances

In a manufacturing organisation, an employee was caught 'red-handed' in the act of falsifying his overtime sheet. This offence was listed as an example of gross misconduct in the company's disciplinary rules and was notorious amongst the workforce as being synonymous with automatic dismissal. The manager involved took precedents into account in reaching his decision to dismiss, although he was also concerned about the message to the rest of the workforce if he was seen to be more lenient. At the appeals hearing, the panel overturned the dismissal and decided that there were mitigating circumstances that could justify a less severe penalty. They included the fact that the employee had financial problems and a terminally ill wife. Further, this was his first and only offence in 15 years of service. The manager happily accepted this decision.

Case study 10 – reinforce the disciplinary rules and publicise outcomes

In a particularly unpleasant bullying case, the housing department principal of a local authority decided, after a lengthy investigation, to dismiss one of his managers for gross misconduct. His instinct was to 'brush the matter under the carpet' by informing employees that the manager had resigned. He was persuaded by the HR manager, however, that the opposite strategy would be more effective in conveying the message that the council would not tolerate such behaviour in future. With the agreement of the employees who had made complaints about the manager's conduct, the principal openly announced to the staff that the manager had been dismissed. He also reassured them that if they had similar complaints in the future they would be investigated and acted upon.

Monitoring and evaluation

In the table on page 69 we stressed the need to continue to monitor and review individuals who have been disciplined. It is also important to monitor and evaluate the operation of the disciplinary procedure more generally.

There are a number of monitoring mechanisms that can be used, some of which entail revisiting the questions that were addressed at the auditing stage (see above). This will help you to identify any changes or trends in the overall statistics and pinpoint whether there are a number of common causes of disciplinary action and if problems are concentrated within particular functions or teams. Be wary of taking these statistics at face value, though, as an increase in disciplinary appeals, for example, may mean that employees are more aware of their rights rather than that the original disciplinary decisions were unjust.

Periodically, a major review of the disciplinary procedure will be necessary to ensure that it is achieving its aim and that the benefits to the organisation and its employees are being realised (see Chapter 2). A number of tools can be used to measure the employee relations climate, including attitude surveys, statistics on labour turnover and absenteeism, and the number and causes of grievances.

Finally, the operation of your disciplinary procedure should be consistently reviewed to ensure that it is relevant, up to date and reflects changes in employment legislation.

Reference

1 JACKSON T. *Handling Grievances*. London, Chartered Institute of Personnel and Development, 2000, p48.

7

What skills and knowledge are required?

- ☑ Introduction
- ☑ Skills requirements
- ☑ Knowledge requirements
- ☑ Before, during and after the interview
- ☑ References

Introduction

This chapter considers the operation of disciplinary procedures. Many of the skills and knowledge requirements for managers, however, will be the same in capability issues. Best practice training should ideally cover all the roles that managers may play in the disciplinary process, from initial informal warnings and investigations through to formal warnings, dismissal and appeal.

With reference to disciplinary interviews, Pont and Pont[1] say:

> Of all the interviews that managers have to conduct, this is the one they least relish. It should also not be

an everyday occurrence so, unlike interviews where performance can improve with practice, there is little opportunity for practice (unless on a training course) and there is no room for error. The cost of mistakes can be enormous and you may make the situation worse rather than better.

As with many management activities, the key is thorough preparation, which we advocate at each of the stages below.

Skills requirements

Managers must be trained to:

- carry out a thorough investigation and keep accurate records
- conduct disciplinary hearings in a professional manner
- conduct effective appeals hearings to check whether the right decision has been made (and to cure procedural flaws, if necessary).

With regard to the first stage, you will need to employ analytical skills in gathering relevant facts and accompanying documentation. These may include:

- interviewing potential witnesses in a non-judgmental way and taking notes that may then form the basis of witness statements
- analysing video or other evidence such as attendance, cost or quality records, computer monitoring information, correspondence, etc
- perusing the employee's personal file, particularly information on previous disciplinary warnings, performance reviews, personal circumstances, etc.

The aim is to decide whether formal action is required. If not, would alternative actions, such as those mentioned in Chapter 4, be appropriate? If so, and the issue is one of poor performance, is the capability procedure a more appropriate tool?

If you do convene a disciplinary hearing, you will need to listen to the employee's case, seek clarification of the points raised and oversee the questioning and cross-examining of witnesses. The hearing must be conducted in an orderly, unemotional, confidential and impartial manner and all those involved must feel that they have had an opportunity to 'have their say'. You will also need to empathise with the employee when considering any mitigating circumstances. Finally, you will be expected to summarise your conclusions, reach a firm decision – based on objective reasoning – and be prepared to justify that decision.

An important aspect of any disciplinary hearing is taking notes. It is preferable if this is undertaken by a second management representative; the aim is to produce a summary of the discussions that can be agreed by both parties. See *Appendix 2* for a checklist on taking notes of disciplinary interviews.

Finally, if you play a role at the appeals stage, you will again need to employ many of the skills highlighted above. You should note that, depending on the circumstances of the case, the appeals hearing may be:

- a review, ie providing an opportunity to hear the employee's grounds for appeal and examining the decision-making process to see whether the disciplinary action was warranted
- a full rehearing; this will be necessary only in

cases where procedural defects occurred in the earlier stages or where new evidence is now available.

See the ACAS advisory handbook[2] for guidance on how to conduct an appeal hearing.

Knowledge requirements

In summary, managers need knowledge of:

- the disciplinary rules, policy and procedure
- their own role and that of others within the procedure
- other company policies and procedures
- custom and practice
- the individual concerned, eg job duties, attendance, health, training, disciplinary record
- relevant legislation, case law and best practice requirements
- relevant clauses in the contract of employment
- details of precedents, ie decisions made in similar previous cases
- the pros and cons of alternative decisions
- likely repercussions of the final decision.

Before, during and after the interview

Finally, in this chapter, we provide a checklist summarising good practices when engaged in the formal stages of the disciplinary procedure (adapted from Martin and Jackson).[3]

The disciplinary interview

Before

Inform the employee in advance of the nature of the allegations.

Suspend the employee on full pay if this is a case of suspected gross misconduct.

Carry out a thorough investigation and gather facts.

Consider any relevant precedents and the employee's disciplinary record.

Inform the employee, preferably in writing, of the subject matter, time, date, location and nature of the hearing and the right to be accompanied. Provide copies of evidence, such as witness statements, preferably prior to the meeting.

Decide on the sequence or structure of the interview. Invite all the relevant parties.

Ensure that the meeting will be properly constituted according to the procedure, eg in a potential dismissal case, a senior manager must take the decision.

During

Convene the disciplinary hearing and make the necessary introductions.

Explain the purpose of the interview; present the allegations and the evidence.

Request that supporting witnesses give their statements and are prepared to answer questions from both parties.

Listen to the employee or the employee's companion when he or she gives his or her side of the story and allow the employee to call supporting witnesses.

Ask questions of the employee and the employee's witnesses (and allow your management colleagues to do the same).

Take comprehensive notes (or arrange for someone else to do this).

Seek clarification of the key issues.

Give the employee (or companion) the opportunity to reiterate any aspects that he or she wishes to emphasise.

Adjourn the interview to allow consideration of the points raised and any extenuating circumstances (or to allow further investigation).

Consider the appropriate action to be taken.

Reconvene and inform the employee of your decision and the reasons for it. Highlight the change in behaviour needed, if appropriate, and the consequences of a failure to improve in the future.

Specify a review date, if there is to be one.

Inform the employee of the appeals procedure.

Afterwards

Confirm the decision in writing to the employee and write up the notes of the interview. Provide a copy to the employee and place copies of all relevant documents on the personal file. Complete the disciplinary record.

Monitor and review.

Note: Halt the proceedings at any point where it is apparent that:

- the use of the disciplinary procedure is inappropriate and counselling or the capability policy and procedure should be used
- there is no case to be answered by the employee.

References

1 PONT T. *and* PONT G. *Interviewing Skills for Managers.* London, Piatkus, 1998, p130.
2 ACAS. *Discipline at Work. Advisory Handbook.* S.7. London, ACAS, Revised November 2000.
3 MARTIN M. and JACKSON T. *Personnel Practice.* 2nd edn, London, Chartered Institute of Personnel and Development, 2000, p117.

What are the key points?

1 The aim of disciplinary procedures is to help and encourage improvement amongst employees whose conduct or standard of work is unsatisfactory, not to hand out punishments. An early response to a problem may 'nip it in the bud' and save a lot of time, effort and money in the long run.

2 There is no statutory obligation for employers to provide disciplinary procedures but employment tribunal decisions and the ACAS Code have made it virtually impossible to operate within the law without a fair procedure.

3 The contents and scope of disciplinary procedures will depend on a number of factors including the nature, size and culture of the organisation, whether it is unionised or not, and the existence of related policies and procedures.

4 Disciplinary rules must be easy to understand, properly communicated to employees and applied consistently. It should be clear that lists of examples of gross misconduct offences are for information only and are not intended to be exhaustive.

5 Disciplinary procedures should contain informal and

formal stages and include a right to appeal to higher levels of management.

6 Managers must carry out thorough and impartial investigations of disciplinary matters before deciding whether formal action is necessary.

7 Managers should differentiate between issues of conduct and capability; separate capability procedures are recommended for cases where shortfalls in performance are outside the employee's control.

8 Capability procedures have three essential features: consultation with the employee, medical investigation, if applicable, and consideration of alternative employment before a decision to dismiss.

9 Failure to follow the company's disciplinary (or capability) procedure can result in breach-of-contract or unfair dismissal claims and is the most common cause of employers losing such cases.

10 At the conclusion of disciplinary (or capability) hearings, employees should fully understand what is expected of them in terms of improvements to conduct, attendance or performance, and what the consequences will be if these do not happen.

11 Training and guidance must be provided to managers, as it is difficult for them to develop the necessary knowledge and skills for effective handling of disciplinary matters.

12 Managers should review their experiences of handling discipline and be prepared, where necessary, to recommend changes to the disciplinary rules, associated policies and procedures and other management activities in order to prevent similar problems arising in the future.

What else do we need to know?

✔ Further reading
✔ Useful contacts

We hope that the information provided throughout this book has convinced you of the need for new (or revised) formal disciplinary and capability procedures and that the good practice guidelines will help you develop and implement ones suited to your organisation's needs. Before starting this process, you should note that there is a lot more help available to you. Listed below are some suggestions for further reading and useful contacts.

Further reading

The following ACAS publications are available from ACAS Reader (Tel: 01455 852225):

Code of Practice on Disciplinary and Grievance Procedures.
    January 2001.
Discipline at Work. Advisory Handbook. Revised November
    2000.

Self Help Guide. Producing Disciplinary and Grievance Procedures.
   November 2000.
Guide for Small Firms. Getting it right...Discipline at work.
   November 1997.
Guide for Small Firms. Getting it right...Tackling absence
   problems. January 1997.
The Role of ACAS. August 1999.
Preventing and Resolving Collective Disputes. July 1999.
Providing Information and Advice. July 1999.
Individual Employment Rights. September 1998.

Other useful publications include:

DEPARTMENT FOR EDUCATION AND EMPLOYMENT. *Code of Practice for*
   the elimination of discrimination in the field of employment
   against disabled persons or persons who have a disability.
   London, HMSO, 1996.
FOWLER A. *The Disciplinary Interview.* London, Institute of
   Personnel and Development, 1998.

Useful contacts

Advisory Conciliation and Arbitration Service (ACAS). There
are 11 regional public enquiry points – see your telephone
directory.

Centre for Dispute Resolution (CEDR). A leading inter-
national organisation in the field of alternative dispute
resolution. Tel: 020 7600 0500.
E-mail: mediate@cedr.co.uk
Website: www.cedr.co.uk

Chartered Institute of Personnel and Development (CIPD, formerly IPD). Tel: 020 8971 9000.
E-mail: cipd@cipd.co.uk
Website: www.cipd.co.uk

Citizens' Advice Bureaux. Locally based – see your telephone directory.

Appendix 1: Example disciplinary procedure

Barbour Index: Disciplinary policy, principles and procedure

Policy

The Company aims to ensure that there will be a fair and consistent approach to the enforcement of standards of conduct throughout the Company. This policy and procedure is designed to help and encourage all employees to achieve and maintain standards of conduct, attendance and job performance. The Company rules, which are summarised in the employees' statements of terms and condition, the staff handbook, this procedure and associated documentation, apply to all employees.

Principles

a) No disciplinary action will be taken against an employee until the case has been fully investigated and a disciplinary interview has taken place.

b) At every stage in the procedure the employee will be advised of the nature of the complaint against him or her and will be given the opportunity to state his or her case before any decision is made.

c) At all stages the employee will have the right to be accompanied by a colleague, lay or trade union official during the investigation, disciplinary interview or disciplinary appeal.

d) In reaching decisions on appropriate disciplinary penalties, managers will take into account any mitigating circumstances.

e) No employee will be dismissed for a first breach of discipline except in the case of gross misconduct when the penalty will be summary dismissal, ie dismissal without notice or pay in lieu of notice.

f) An employee will have the right to appeal against any disciplinary penalty imposed to a higher level of management.

g) The procedure may be implemented at any stage if the employee's alleged misconduct warrants such action.

h) In poor performance cases, where the reason is not within the control of the employee, eg health, training or the changing nature of the job, the Company's Capability Policy and Procedure will be used in place of this procedure. However, poor performance resulting from, for example, negligence, lack of application or attitudinal problems will be dealt with under the disciplinary procedure. Further, where an employee's absence record has been investigated and the absences are deemed to be of casual nature, the employee will be dealt with under the disciplinary procedure.

Procedure

Minor faults will be dealt with informally by line managers, but where the matter is more serious the following procedure may be used:

Stage 1 – Oral warning

If your conduct or performance does not meet acceptable standards, you will normally be given a formal oral warning by your immediate manager. You will be advised of the reason for the warning, that it is the first stage of the disciplinary procedure and of your right of appeal. A record will be kept of the oral warning and placed on your file. The warning will be disregarded for disciplinary purposes after six months, subject to your satisfactory conduct and performance.

Stage 2 – Written warning

If the offence is a serious one, or if a further offence or no improvement occurs within six months of the oral warning, a written warning will be given to you by your immediate manager. This will give details of the complaint, the improvement required and the timescale. It will warn you that, if there is no satisfactory improvement, further disciplinary action may be taken and will advise of your right of appeal. A copy of this written warning will be placed on your file but will be disregarded for disciplinary purposes after nine months, subject to your satisfactory conduct and performance.

Stage 3 – Final written warning

If there is still a failure to improve conduct or performance is still unsatisfactory, or if your misconduct is sufficiently serious to warrant only one written warning but insufficiently serious to justify dismissal (in effect both first and final written warning), a final written warning will normally be given to you by your manager. This will give details of the complaint, will warn that dismissal will result if there is no satisfactory improvement and will advise of the right of appeal. A copy of this final written warning will be placed on your file but will be disregarded for disciplinary purposes after 12 months (in exceptional cases the period may be longer), subject to your satisfactory conduct and performance.

Stage 4 – Dismissal

If conduct or performance is still unsatisfactory and you fail to reach the prescribed standards, dismissal will normally result. Only an appropriate senior manager can take a decision to dismiss. You will be provided, as soon as reasonably practicable, with written reasons for dismissal, the date on which your employment will terminate (in accordance with your notice entitlement) and will be notified of your right of appeal.

Alternatives short of dismissal may be considered. They are:

a) demotion to a more suitable job, if available

b) transfer to other departments and/or duties.

Gross misconduct

If you are accused of gross misconduct, the Company may suspend you from work on full pay, normally for no more than five working days, while it investigates the alleged offence. The Company will explain its reasons in writing to you. During any period of suspension, you shall not attend your place of work other than for the purpose of attending disciplinary proceedings, including investigatory hearings. Nor shall you contact any other employees, suppliers or customers of the Company, except your companion, without the Company's consent.

Examples of gross misconduct are:

- theft, fraud, bribery (giving and receiving)
- unauthorised entry to computer records or deliberate falsification of records
- a serious breach of the Company's rules on e-mail and Internet usage
- fighting or assault
- deliberate or reckless damage to Company property
- inability to perform your duties through being under the influence of alcohol or drugs
- a serious breach of the Company's safety rules or a single error due to negligence which causes or could have caused significant loss, damage or injury to the Company, its employees or customers
- conviction of a criminal offence which makes you unsuitable or unable to carry out your duties
- a serious act of insubordination such as deliberate refusal to carry out proper instructions
- acts of bullying, harassment or discrimination
- a serious breach of trust or confidentiality.

This list is not intended to be an exhaustive one and only gives an indication of the types of offences that may be considered to be gross misconduct.

If, on completion of the investigation and the full disciplinary procedure, the Company is satisfied that gross misconduct has occurred, the result will normally be summary dismissal without notice or pay in lieu of notice.

Disciplinary investigations

The Company is committed to ensuring that all potential infringements of disciplinary rules are fully investigated. This may entail carrying out interviews with the employee concerned and third parties such as witnesses, colleagues and managers as well as analysing written records and information. It may also involve a search of your person and/or property. The investigation report will be made available to all the parties concerned. Where necessary, the identity of witnesses will be kept confidential.

Where an employee is called to attend an investigatory interview, it will be made clear that this is not a disciplinary hearing.

Appeals

If you wish to appeal against a disciplinary decision, you must do so through your immediate manager within two working days of the receipt of the disciplinary letter. The appeal should be made in writing, stating the ground(s) on which the disciplinary penalty should be reviewed.

A manager or director senior to the one who made the original decision will hear the appeal. In the rare circumstances where this is not possible, alternative arrangements will be agreed with you and your companion.

The appeals hearing will be normally held within five working days of receipt of the letter. The decision of the senior manager or director (or authorised deputy) shall be final.

The appeals hearing

At the appeals hearing, the employee will be given full opportunity to state the ground(s) on which the appeal is made. The disciplining manager will then have the opportunity to explain his or her decision to impose the given penalty. The manager or director conducting the appeal may exercise discretion as to whether or not the two parties will be present together or separately during the proceedings.

When all the evidence has been heard the hearing will be adjourned. The manager or director conducting the appeal will consider the merits of the appeal, in private, before reaching a decision.

1 The manager/director of the appeal hearing will, whenever possible, inform the employee orally of the decision reached and confirm this in writing no later than seven working days after the hearing.

2 The manager/director of the appeal hearing has the authority to quash or reduce a disciplinary penalty or, in exceptional and appropriate circumstances, to increase it, in accordance with the penalties specified in the company's disciplinary procedure.

3 Employees should note that an appeal hearing is not intended to repeat the detailed investigation that led to or formed part of the disciplinary hearing, but to focus on specific factors which the employee feels have received insufficient consideration, such as:

- an inconsistent/inappropriate harsh penalty
- extenuating circumstances
- bias of the disciplining manager
- unfairness of the hearing
- new evidence subsequently coming to light.

4 Where an appeal against dismissal fails, the effective date of termination shall be the date on which the employee was originally dismissed.

Last updated: 8.3.01

Appendix 2: Checklist for taking notes of disciplinary interviews

The following checklist should assist you in ensuring that your written notes fully meet the need to:

- provide sufficient information to whomever is responsible for issuing the confirmation letter to the employee (if this is necessary)
- provide a useful justification and record of the action taken at this stage should the situation deteriorate further (possibly resulting in an unfair dismissal claim being heard at an employment tribunal).

Do the notes include: YES/NO

1 the date, venue and start time of the interview?
2 an account of those attending the interview and their roles?
3 details of the allegations stated to the employee and of the supporting evidence, eg witness statements in writing?

YES/NO

4 details of the employee's response and of the
supporting evidence?

5 a record of any adjournments and approximate
timings?

6 consideration of the employee's previous record?

7 the decision on whether disciplinary action was
appropriate or not and the type of action taken,
the reasons for it and the appropriate timescale?

8 the review date and a clear statement of intent
if improvement does not occur?

9 reference to the right to appeal and the finish
time of the interview?

10 reference to the note-taker's name plus a date
and signature?

Appendix 3: Example capability procedure
Reigate and Banstead Council
Work Capability Procedure

1. PRINCIPLES

1.1 This procedure is designed to deal with those cases where the employee is lacking in some area of knowledge, skill or ability, resulting in a failure to be able to carry out the required duties to an acceptable standard. It is to be used where there is a genuine lack of capability, rather than a deliberate failure on the part of the employee to perform to the standards of which (s)he is capable (for which use of the disciplinary procedure is appropriate). A genuine lack of capability may have been present for some time or may have come about more recently because of, for example, changing job content or personal factors affecting the individual's performance.

1.2 The procedure seeks to:
   a) assist employees to improve their performance, wherever possible, when such deficiencies exist
   b) provide a firm but fair and consistent means

97

of dealing with capability problems without employing the disciplinary procedure

c) provide means of solving incapability problems where improvement in the current job is not possible.

1.3 Accompanying this procedure is a set of guidance notes designed to explain how the procedure should be applied. Interpretation of the application of elements of the procedure must be carried out in conjunction with these notes.

2. APPLICATION

2.1 The procedure applies to all employees of Reigate and Banstead Borough Council.

3. INFORMAL ASSISTANCE

3.1 Nothing in this procedure is intended to prevent the normal process of supervisory control whereby line managers allocate work, monitor performance, draw attention to errors and poor quality and highlight work done well. This may include informal assistance in achieving improvement.

3.2 Much of this will be carried out in conjunction with the appraisal process where discussions should be consistent with indications of under-performance. Such methods are not part of the formal capability procedure, and therefore formal interviews and representation are not appropriate to this everyday process. Line managers should maintain personal notes of difficulties encountered, assistance given and any remedial actions taken for future reference in case formal action is needed; the employee is entitled to have a copy of such notes.

4. REPRESENTATION

4.1 At all stages of the formal procedure an employee is entitled to have a representative present, who may be a fellow employee or a trade union representative. It will be made clear in advance to the employee (and to the representative, if the employee exercises this option) that the capability rather than the disciplinary procedure is being used.

4.2 If at any stage a line manager has reason to believe that the under-performance is due to poor conduct or lack of effort on the part of the employee, (s)he will stop the process and may set up a disciplinary interview at a later date in accordance with that procedure. (S)he will inform the employee clearly of the change of procedure and repeat that there is a right to representation if this has not previously been taken up.

5. THE FORMAL PROCEDURE

5.1 Stage 1 – Formal counselling

5.1.1 Where an employee is failing to perform to an acceptable standard despite having been given informal guidance and assistance, a formal counselling session will be arranged with him/her line manager giving at least two working days' written notice of the interview, which will include:

a) the procedure and stage being used
b) clear details of the shortfall in performance
c) all necessary supporting documentation
d) details of any informal action taken so far
e) the right of representation.

5.1.2 During this counselling the employee will be told clearly of the deficiencies which have been identified and precisely of the improvement in work standard which is required (with the possible consequences of not doing so). There must be an opportunity for the employee to answer these points and to explain any difficulties which s(he) may be having, and a discussion on the ways and means by which the desired improvement may be achieved. Appropriate possibilities would include:

i) training, either external or internal
ii) working under closer supervision from a line manager, or a work colleague who is competent and experienced in the work, for an agreed specified period
iii) agreed changes in duties, either permanently or for a trial period.

5.1.3 The conclusions from this counselling session will be formally recorded in writing with a copy given to the employee within five working days of the meeting. The employee will also be given details of the right of appeal.

5.1.4 A reasonable timescale for improvements will be set (length to be determined by individual circumstances but normally not longer than three months), with monitoring during that period. If the desired improvement has been achieved, a meeting will be convened with the employee and (s)he will be apprised of the situation. This will be recorded and the employee will be given a copy of the file note.

5.2 **Stage 2 – Formal review meeting**

5.2.1 If the desired improvement has not been achieved, the employee will be clearly told of the continued areas of under-performance by his/her Service Manager in the same manner as at paragraph 5.1.1.

5.2.2 The remedial measures previously identified will also be reviewed, and there will be discussion on whether they should continue or if additional measures might be helpful. The employee will again be afforded the right to answer the points made and explain his/her problems.

5.2.3 It may be felt appropriate at this stage to discuss formal career counselling or whether a permanent redeployment would be possible and, if so, an agreeable option for the employee. This may be particularly appropriate for an employee who has not been able to cope with a promotion but was satisfactory in the previous job. If this is an agreed possibility the Personnel Manager will be notified and the further steps required to attempt to implement this solution will be under his/her control. (The redeployment policy will be applied in approved cases but where there is redeployment to a post on a lower grade, there will be no salary protection.)

5.2.4 The review meeting will be followed by a formal letter to the employee setting out the continued deficiencies, the expected improvement, the timescale for achieving it, the further help which will be given, any agreed changes to the employment contract and that a failure to achieve the improvement within the timescale will necessitate a consideration of whether employment should be terminated. It therefore acts as a final warning letter, and the Personnel Manager should be formally notified in writing to ensure (s)he is aware of the action taken; it will also set out the employee's right of appeal, including to whom it should be made and the time limited for doing so (see paragraph 7).

5.2.5 A reasonable timescale for improvement will be set (again normally not longer than three months), with monitoring during that period. If the desired improvement has been achieved, this will be recorded at a meeting with the employee and (s)he will be given a copy of the file note confirming the situation.

5.3   **Stage 3 – Final resolution**

5.3.1 If the desired improvement has still not been achieved, a meeting must be held by the employee's Director (or other nominated Officer), and the Personnel Manager (or his/her representative) when the employee will again be clearly told of the continued deficiencies in the same manner as at paragraph 5.1.1. After the employee has been offered the opportunity to answer the points made, the Director will make a decision as to whether there is any likelihood of the employee's performance achieving an acceptable level by extending the assistance offered and timescale allowed under the previous stage.

5.3.2 If the decision is that performance will not become acceptable in the current post, a further consideration of whether permanent redeployment (at the same or lower pay level) is possible, and of whether the alternative job is likely to be performed acceptably by the employee, will be made.

5.3.3 In cases where an employee has been performing satisfactorily but the job has changed significantly and the employee cannot cope, or where an employee has been recently over-promoted, the Service Committee may recommend that the Personnel Committee approve an efficiency retirement where this is a mutually acceptable solution.

5.3.4 In addition or as an alternative the facility of 'out-placement' may be offered on terms to be agreed having regard to the merits of the particular case. The cost of the out-placement will be offset against the level of approved efficiency retirement if appropriate.

5.3.5 If no suitable alternative employment is available, or the employee declines redeployment or an efficiency termination, dismissal will take place. The fact of and reasons for the dismissal, the last date of employment, any necessary administrative or financial arrangements, and to whom, and within what time limit, any appeal should be made, will be confirmed to the employee in writing within five working days (see paragraph 6 below).

6. APPEALS

6.1 An appeal right exists at all stages of the formal procedure. There will not be a delay in implementing management decisions pending the appeal, but they may be subsequently amended as a result of the appeal hearing.

6.2 Appeals must be lodged with the Personnel Manager within seven working days of receipt of either a letter of formal action or a termination of employment letter, and the appeal hearing must take place within the next 20 working days (unless the parties agree to a delay). The employee has the same right of representation at an appeal as during the above formal stages.

6.3 Appeals at Stage 1 will be heard by an Officer senior to the Officer who conducted the interview, or the departmental director.

6.4 Appeals at Stage 2 will be heard by the departmental Director (or, in the event of their involvement in the case, an alternative Director).

6.5 Appeals at Stage 3 will be heard by the Appeals Panel of the Personnel Committee.

6.6 The procedure to be followed at all stages of appeal will be the same as for the disciplinary procedure.

7. CAPABILITY OF SERVICE MANAGERS, DIRECTORS AND THE LEAD DIRECTOR

7.1 The principles and procedures in the preceding paragraphs apply to Business Unit Managers, Directors and the Lead Director as much as to other employees, but the stages in their cases will need to be undertaken at different levels. For Service Managers all stages within the procedure will be undertaken by the departmental Director, with Stage 1 and 2 appeals heard by the Lead Director.

7.2 Each stage of the capability procedure for Directors and the Lead Director will be conducted by Panels of Members convened in accordance with their equivalent levels in their disciplinary procedure.